EXPLORE
ANCIENT
WORLDS

ANCIENT
ASSYRIA

KATHLEEN TRACY

Mitchell Lane
PUBLISHERS

P.O. Box 196
Hockessin, Delaware 19707
Visit us on the web: www.mitchelllane.com
Comments? email us: contactus@mitchelllane.com

Ancient Assyria • Ancient Athens
The Aztecs • Ancient Babylon
The Byzantine Empire • The Celts of the British Isles
Ancient China • Ancient Egypt
Ancient India/Maurya Empire • Ancient Sparta

ABOUT THE AUTHOR: Journalist and children's
book author Kathleen Tracy is an avid sports
fan who lives in Southern California with her
two dogs and African gray parrot.

PUBLISHER'S NOTE: The facts on which the story
in this book is based have been thoroughly
researched. Documentation of such research
can be found on page 45. While every possible
effort has been made to ensure accuracy, the
publisher will not assume liability for damages
caused by inaccuracies in the data, and
makes no warranty on the accuracy of the
information contained herein.

Printing 1 2 3 4 5 6 7 8 9

Library of Congress
Cataloging-in-Publication Data
Tracy, Kathleen.
  Ancient Assyria / by Kathleen Tracy.
    p. cm.—(Explore ancient worlds)
  Includes bibliographical references and index.
  ISBN 978-1-61228-282-4 (library bound)
  1. Assyria—Civilization—Juvenile literature. 2.
Assyria—History—Juvenile literature. I. Title.
  DS73.2.T72 2013
  935'.03—dc23
                                    2012015878

eBook ISBN: 9781612283579

PLB

CONTENTS

Nineveh represented at the height of its power.

CHAPTER 1

The Battle of Carchemish

For hundreds of years, the ancient Assyrians and Babylonians lived side by side. But it was not a peaceful relationship. During this time, the two kingdoms fought numerous wars. Sometimes Assyria was victorious; other times Babylon won and asserted its authority over Assyria—until the next war. Back and forth it went as each kingdom sought to control the region between the Tigris and Euphrates Rivers, which is known as Mesopotamia.

Eventually, the rivalry between Assyria and Babylon came down to one pivotal battle. Near the end of the seventh century BCE, Babylon had grown very powerful. In 612 BCE, its ruler Nabopolassar sacked Assyria's capital city, Nineveh. Nineveh was Assyria's oldest and most populous city. Originally settled around 5000 BCE, Nineveh eventually became an important religious center. King Sennacherib, who was the Assyrian ruler from 704–681 BCE, made it the capital. Sennacherib built large walls around the city to protect it from its enemies. Unfortunately, the walls weren't enough to save it from the Babylonians.

Two years later after the destruction of Nineveh, the Babylonians captured the new Assyrian capital of Harran. Once again the Assyrians were forced to relocate their capital, this time to Carchemish, located on the west banks of the Euphrates River in what is now modern-day Turkey.

Babylon's victories were not just bad news for Assyrian king Ashur-uballit II. The Egyptian pharaoh, Necho II, was also concerned about

Babylon's westward expansion, which threatened to block lucrative trade routes. It was in the best interests of both Assyria and Egypt to stop Babylon from getting any more powerful than it already was. So when Ashur-uballit II sent a message asking Necho for military aid, the pharaoh agreed to join forces against Babylon.

The plan was for Necho to gather his army and march northward to meet up with the Assyrian forces at Carchemish and help defend their newest capital. To reach Carchemish, Necho needed to pass through territory controlled by the Judeans. Some historians believe that the Judean king Josiah had aligned his kingdom with Babylon. Others suggest Josiah was simply trying to assert his power against Egypt. Whatever his motivation, Josiah denied Necho permission to pass through Judah and had his army block the Egyptians' way. The subsequent events are recounted in the Bible:

Prior to the Battle of Carchemish, Egypt's army was considered one of the greatest in the then-known world. But after Nebuchadnezzar defeated the Assyrians and their allies, Egypt's army was decimated and Babylon became the undisputed conqueror of ancient Mesopotamia.

King Josiah shot by arrows

While Josiah was king, Pharaoh Neco, king of Egypt, went to the Euphrates River to help the king of Assyria. King Josiah and his army marched out to fight him, but King Neco killed him when they met at Megiddo. (2 Kings 23:29)[1]

After all this, when Josiah had set the temple in order, Neco king of Egypt came up to make war at Carchemish on the Euphrates, and Josiah went out to engage him. But Neco sent messengers to him, saying, "What have we to do with each other, O King of Judah? I am not coming against you today but against the house with which I am at war, and God has ordered me to hurry. Stop for your own sake from interfering with God who is with me, so that He will not destroy you." (2 Chronicles 35:20-24) [2]

A battle ensued at the city of Megiddo between Necho's army and Josiah's soldiers. During the fighting, Josiah was gravely wounded by an Egyptian archer and taken back to Jerusalem, where he died.

Bronze statue of Necho II

When the Egyptians finally arrived at Carchemish, they teamed up with the Assyrians and marched on Harran. But the Babylonians weathered the attack and drove the attackers back to Carchemish. On his way back to Egypt, Necho captured the newly named King of Judah, Josiah's son Johoahaz, and installed his older brother Eliakim as a puppet king, renaming him Jehoiakim. Necho took Jehoahaz to Egypt and imprisoned him.

Over the next few years, Babylonia continued to take over more territory along the Euphrates River. Once again, Necho geared up for battle against the Babylonian army, now led by crown prince Nebuchadnezzar. In late spring 605 BC, the pharaoh and the Assyrian forces engaged the Babylonians at Carchemish. Nebuchadnezzar led his troops to a decisive victory against the Assyrian and Egyptian armies. What was left of the pharaoh's army retreated. The Babylonians pursued and killed the rest of the Egyptian soldiers.

It was a turning point in Middle Eastern history. The battle wiped out Egypt's military might, made Babylon the undisputed power in the Middle East, and marked the end of the Assyrian Empire. But the contributions of the Assyrian civilization are still evident today.

Assyria and the Bible

Assyria is frequently mentioned in the Bible, giving it an interesting perspective on the culture's history and influences. For example, archaeologists who have tried to find the historical inspiration for the Garden of Eden are given some tantalizing clues in the Bible that this paradise on Earth lay in or around Assyria.

King Shalmaneser V

> *A river watering the garden flowed from Eden, and from there it divided. It had four headstreams. The name of the first is the Pishon. It winds through the entire land of Havilah, where there is gold. The gold of that land is good; aromatic resin and onyx are also there. The name of the second river is the Gihon; it winds through the entire land of Cush. The name of the third river is the Tigris; it runs along the east side of Assur. And the fourth river is the Euphrates. (Genesis 2:8-14)[3]*

Perhaps Assyria's most notable role in Biblical history came when it conquered Israel under the leadership of King Shalmaneser V during the eighth century BCE. Typically, Assyria's policy to prevent revolt in conquered territories was to deport many members of the native population to other regions. In keeping with this policy, Assyria exiled the ten tribes of the Kingdom of Israel: Reuben, Simeon, Dan, Naphtali, Gad, Asher, Issachar, Zebulon, Ephraim, and Manasseh. Some historians believe these tribes were exiled to what is now modern-day Syria and Iraq, but what actually became of the tribes after Assyria conquered Israel remains one of history's unsolved mysteries.

Tigris River At Diyarbakir

CHAPTER 2

Brief History

The ancient region known as Mesopotamia was the area located between the Tigris and Euphrates rivers. Mesopotamia included the modern countries of Iraq, Syria, Lebanon, Israel, Jordan, Palestine, and Kuwait, and the Sinai Peninsula. The area is also called the Cradle of Civilization because the world's first civilization developed there.

According to historians, a civilization is defined as a culture that has a system of recordkeeping and has developed specialization to address the economic, social, religious, and political needs of the citizens, such as an artisan class—artists who create works that reflect the community—and architecture.

More than seven thousand years ago, around 5000 BCE, a group of settlers arrived in southern Mesopotamia. Historians are not sure where they came from but these people built permanent settlements, constructing homes built of sun-dried bricks made of mud and straw. They survived by developing a system of agriculture, with yearly seasons of plowing, seeding, and harvesting. Although this region of the world does not get much rainfall, the land between the Tigris and Euphrates has channels filled with fish and extensive marshland layered with silt from regular flooding. Because of these favorable conditions, the area is also called the Fertile Crescent.

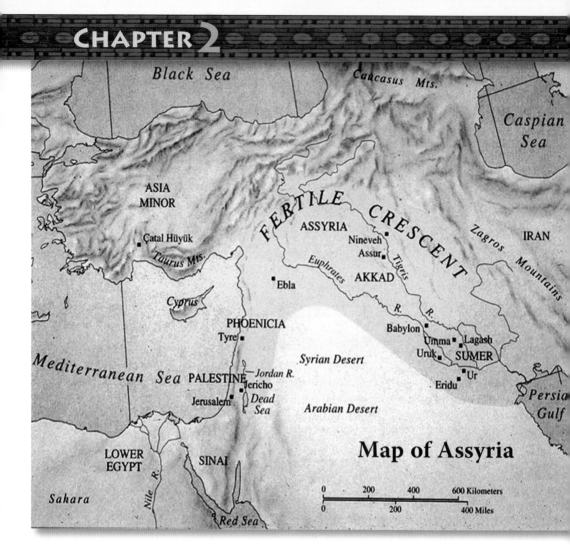

Map of Assyria

The lower part of this region, nearest where the rivers converge near the western end of the Persian Gulf, was comprised of two areas: Akkad in the north and Sumer in the south by the river delta. Over the next 1,500 years or so, the Sumerians drained the swampy land to make it suitable for farming, learned to control the flooding, and built irrigation canals.

It is estimated that sometime between 3500 BCE and 3100 BCE, the Sumerian culture laid the foundations "for a type of economy and social order markedly different from anything previously known. This far more complex culture, based on large urban centers rather than simple villages, is what we associate with civilization."[1]

Sumer was first ruled by priests, then later by kings who were regarded as gods. The kingdom was eventually organized into city-states, the best known of which was Ur. The Sumerians remained a prosperous and strong civilization up until around 2000 BCE.

Directly north of Sumer, where the Tigris and Euphrates run close together, was Akkad. This area had less flooding but was still agriculturally fertile from rainfall and irrigation. This region was first inhabited by a series of Semitic peoples, including the Amorites, who conquered the area about 2000 BCE and established the city of Babylon. As a result, the area was known afterward as Babylonia, which would play a vital role in Mesopotamia for well over a thousand years.

A third region in Mesopotamia that extended from north of Babylonia to the Taurus Mountain range in modern-day Turkey was called Assyria. It had rolling hills that were irrigated by a large number of streams flowing from the surrounding mountains, along with the headwaters of the Tigris and Euphrates. The Assyrians were also a Semitic people, who were especially warlike, similar to the Spartans of Greece. They appear in historical records beginning around 2300 BCE, when Akkad invaded their then-small kingdom. Three hundred years later the Assyrians had established themselves as successful traders who traveled regularly between their capital city of Assur and southern Turkey, trading textiles and tin for gold, silver, and other metals. After the Hittites conquered Turkey around 1800 BCE, this trade route was abandoned.

From 1700 BCE to 1360 BCE, Assyria was controlled by a number of other cultures until the Assyrian governor of Assur, Ashur-uballit, named himself the King of Assyria and successfully waged war to regain independence. Around 1225 BCE, under the rule of King Tukulti-Ninurta I—who is mentioned in the Biblical book of Genesis with the name of Nimrod—the Assyrians conquered the city of Babylon. He was killed, probably in 1208, when his palace was set on fire by citizens upset over Tukulti's plundering of Babylon's religious icons.

Mesopotamia subsequently suffered through a Dark Age, caused by a widespread drought, famine, a decline in population, and a loss of infrastructure. The Assyrians weathered the difficulties better than its neighbors so as the Dark Age ended they were able to expand their

An Assyrian chairiot

kingdom. During the reign of Tiglath-Pileser I (1115–1076 BCE), they once again controlled Babylonia and other areas to the west.

Initially, Assyrian military campaigns were basically looting excursions. The army would march south every spring along the Tigris River, go across to the Euphrates, and then follow that upstream until the troops returned to Assur, typically toward the end of summer.

Shalmaneser III was more ambitious and sought to expand the Assyrian empire further west and south, to the Jewish kingdoms of Israel and Judah. By 830 BC, Shalmaneser had succeeded in having pro-Assyrian leaders running both kingdoms. But in 827 BC, near the end of Shalmaneser's reign, there was a great revolt at the Assyrian city of Nineveh, led by the king's son, Assur-danin-pal. The uprising was eventually quelled but it weakened the military enough that the planned annual looting missions were disbanded.

In 744 BCE, Tiglath-Pileser III came to power and is credited with establishing the Assyrian Empire. During his rule, he conquered Syria and Palestine, and merged Babylonia with Assyria. He consolidated his power by forcing conquered people to relocate from their homeland to Assyria. Transplanting people assimilated them into the Assyrian community and made them dependent on local authority.

Tiglath-Pileser III is considered the founder of the Assyrian empire. He used a combination of diplomacy, a strong army, and the relocation of conquered people to expand Assyria's power.

Tiglath-Pileser III died in 727 BC. Within 20 years, the Assyrians ruled most of Mesopotamia and even controlled Egypt. But rather than try to expand their empire even more, the Assyrian leaders who followed Tiglath spent their resources on maintaining services and infrastructure to keep the people under their rule content. They built roads, established courts, constructed bridges, promoted education, and supported culture. Sennacherib (704–681 BCE), for example, developed new irrigation equipment, discovered new mineral veins, established Nineveh as the new Assyrian capital and filled it with parks, and constructed a new aqueduct to make sure the city had plenty of fresh water.

The last few kings were not able to maintain the empire. Esarhaddon (680–669 BCE) tried to assimilate Egypt into the empire, straining the Assyrian army's resources. He also instituted a new policy where he gave Assyria to his son Ashurbanipal (668–627 BCE) and Babylonia to another son. This decision would eventually lead to civil war between the two brothers. After Ashurbanipal captured Babylon in 648 BCE, his position

Statue of King Ashurbanipal

seemed superficially as strong as ever, so that between then and the end of the civil war in 639 BCE, it seemed that Assyria had once again confirmed its power.

But the demographics of Mesopotamia and the surrounding area were changing. New groups had moved into the area, such as the Medes, an Indo-European race. After the Babylonian king Nabopolassar—Nebuchadnezzar's father—made an alliance with the Medes, the days of the Assyrian Empire were numbered. Less than 50 years after Ashurbanipal's victory in Babylon, the Assyrian Empire would come to an end.

Cuneiform

One of the first known writing systems was developed by the Sumerians. Called cuneiform, it was originally a series of pictographs, which are pictorial symbols for a word or phrase. The No Smoking sign with a red line through a cigarette is an example of a pictograph. Over time, cuneiform became a series of wedge-shaped symbols written on clay tablets

Cuneiform writing

with a stylus made out of wood, metal, or a reed. Later cultures, including Babylon and Assyria, adopted cuneiform.

Early Assyrians spoke the Akkadian language which was a Northeastern Semitic language used between 3000 BCE–1000 BCE. It had two dialects—Assyrian and Babylonian—which is why it is also known as Assyro-Babylonian. Akkadian was written in cuneiform along with Aramaic, Persian and other Middle Eastern languages. After around 700 BCE, Aramaic gradually started to replace Akkadian and by 200 AD, it had become an extinct language. The last known example of cuneiform dates from 75 AD.

The Aramaic spoken by the late Assyrians was written in both the Aramaic script as well as the cuneiform script so both styles survived the historical record. However, for many centuries the Sumerians and their language were forgotten until an inscription was discovered in Behistun, Iran. It had been engraved on a cliff 300 feet above the ground by Persian King Darius the Great, extolling his military victories. The inscription was written in three scripts: old Persian cuneiform, Babylonian, and Elamite, enabling researchers—starting in the nineteenth century—to decipher the cuneiform and helping establish the field of Assyriology, the historical and linguistic study of cultures that used cuneiform.

Men and women were not treated
as equals in ancient Assyria

CHAPTER 3

Law and Order

Not surprisingly, Assyrian laws were similar to codes established in Sumer and Babylon. They covered crimes such as property theft and murder. But they also had many laws focused on social customs of the time, such as how women were supposed to act, or not act, toward men. Some of the punishments seem particularly gruesome, such as having one's eyes gouged out or body parts cut off. There was also capital punishment.

While no complete legal code for Assyria has been discovered, three different collections of Assyrian laws have been located by archeologists and historians. The earliest known Code of the Assyrians was established during the reign of Tiglath-Pileser I. Some of the laws in this code include the following:

If a woman brings her hand against a man, they shall prosecute her; 30 manas of lead shall she pay, 20 blows shall they inflict on her.

If a man divorce his wife, if he wish, he may give her something; if he does not wish, he need not give her anything. Empty shall she go out.

If a man meddle with the field of his neighbor, they shall convict him. Threefold shall he restore. One of his fingers they shall cut off, a hundred blows they shall inflict upon him, one month of days he shall do the king's work.

If a man brings his hand against the wife of a man…one of his fingers they shall cut off. If he kisses her, they shall cut off his lower lip with the blade of an axe.

Unless it is forbidden in the tablets, a man may strike his wife, pull her hair, her ear he may bruise or pierce. He commits no misdeed thereby.[1]

Practicing magic was punishable by death. And there is an indication that honor killings were permissible, in which a woman could be put to death by her father or other male relatives if she brought shame to the family name.

Beyond codes for criminal punishments, there are also records to show a well-established civil legal code, including evidence of court-like decisions, business contracts, and other legal documents signed in front of witnesses and archived in the kingdom's records.

The Assyrian king, who lived in the city of Assur, was considered their god Ashur's representative on earth. In addition to being Ashur's high priest, the king was also commander of the army and made all the decisions regarding foreign policy and domestic issues. In general, Assyria could be called a theocracy because the king believed he was acting on behalf of god. Kings were expected to expand the kingdom and whenever the Assyrian troops went on missions to capture other areas or cities, it was considered part of a holy war against those who did not accept and worship Ashur.

To further that goal, the Assyrians established the strongest army not just in Mesopotamia, but also in the entire ancient world. Their military might at its peak would be matched only by the Roman army several centuries later. Early in its history, the army was comprised of peasants recruited to serve. Later, the Assyrian army became more professional, with structured training. The army also included mercenaries, professional soldiers for hire. It is estimated that at its peak, the Assyrian army may have had up to 200,000 men.

Like the Spartans of Greece, the military leaders were often nobles and soldiers were held in the highest esteem. And war and conquest was an integral part of their cultural identity. The walls of the king's palace were decorated with bas-reliefs, a kind of carving, which showed pictures of war victories.

Assyrian solders were well-equipped. They were the first to use spears and arrows made with iron, which would easily go through their opponents' shields. They also put iron tips on their battering rams for extra strength. Their archers were among the best trained and most accurate in the ancient world. Their arrows could travel nearly the length of three football fields. The foot soldiers also used sling shots with deadly accuracy along with swords, spears, and javelins.

They also used sturdy, horse-drawn chariots that held the driver and an archer. Over time, they added a second archer who protected the chariot from a rear attack. But chariots were not as effective on hilly or uneven ground. So the Assyrians also developed a cavalry, where two soldiers rode

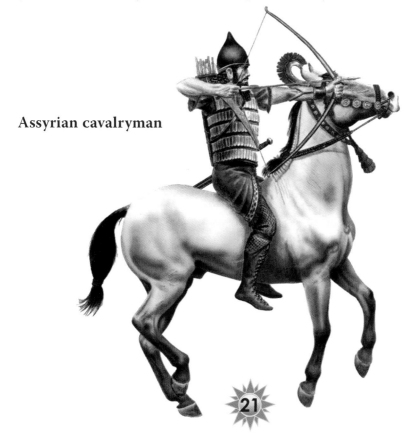

Assyrian cavalryman

Assyrians attack and break through the walls of an enemy city

side by side. One would control the reins of both animals, while the second was an archer or a spearman who wore a shield on his back as armor.

For all their firepower, the Assyrians would give their opponents the chance to surrender before launching an all-out assault. First, a representative for the king would visit the opponent's leader and suggest they surrender without bloodshed. If that leader refused, the Assyrians then surrounded the city, calling out for the citizens to surrender. If they continued to resist, the Assyrians would attack and break through the city's walls. The soldiers would engage in horrible brutality to some of their captives to keep the rest in line. If some dared to rebel or even resist, they could be uprooted from their homes and sent to another part of the empire, never to see their friends and family again. In short, it was rule by intimidation.

After conquering a city or region, the soldiers expected to be given gifts called tributes, which could be anything: gold, art, pottery, and even slaves. If the goods were not given freely, the soldiers simply took them.

In the end, the Assyrians were victims of their empire's success. They ended up controlling such a large expanse of territory that it spread their military too thin, making it difficult to police and maintain order. Eventually, opponents were able to defeat the weakened army, setting the stage for the empire's eventual downfall.

Hammurabi and His Code

Hammurabi

Many of the laws of Assyria were derived from Babylonian laws. These were developed by Hammurabi, who ruled between 1792–1750 BCE and united much of Mesopotamia.

Hammurabi respected the law and expected citizens to follow the codes. His laws applied to everyone—the rich would be punished alongside the poor. To make sure everyone knew the laws, Hammurabi had them written down on an eight-foot-tall slab of stone called a stele.

The Code of Hammurabi contains 282 laws. Nearly half focus on business, such as specifying how much various professions should be paid for their services, or other commercial matters. For example, "If a man has caught either a male or female runaway slave in the open field and has brought him back to his owner, the owner of the slave shall give him two shekels of silver."[2]

Many laws take an "eye for an eye" approach to punishment. The punishments were harsh, to make people think twice before breaking the law to better maintain order:

> If a man has borne false witness in a trial, or has not established the statement that he has made, if that case be a capital trial, that man shall be put to death.

> If a man has stolen a child, he shall be put to death.

> If the captor has secreted that slave in his house and afterward that slave has been caught in his possession, he shall be put to death.[3]

Not only was the Code an inspiration for Assyrian law, it is considered to be the predecessor of Jewish and Islamic legal systems as well.

An Assyrian city under construction

Assyrian society was divided into different social classes. The king was at the top, with nobles and high government officials just below him. Other classes included priests, merchants, and artisans. Many if not most Assyrians were farmers, who worked the land for the nobles who owned it.

At the very bottom of the class structure were slaves. Prisoners of war were made slaves. Debtors could also be made slaves but they retained the right to get married, go to court, and own property. Women were not allowed to have careers and were expected to get married, raise their children, and take care of the household.

The houses of common Assyrians were made out of mud bricks and were only one story tall. The villages in the empire were connected by small but serviceable roads. In the major cities, there were large, multi-story buildings such as ziggurats and the king's palace, which often had sculpture and gardens decorating the property. Some of these statues depicted demons, which were intended to protect the building and the town from evil influences.

The upper classes could enjoy hunting parks, along with gardens filled with flowers and plants and irrigated by water canals. The kings lived in ornate palaces and each city built temples where the Assyrians could worship and pay homage to their gods. Just as the Romans adopted their

The second most important god behind Ashur, Ishtar was the Assyrian and Babylonian goddess of war and love. She is often depicted with a lion, which symbolizes her power.

gods from the Greeks, the Assyrian gods were adopted from the Babylonians and the Sumerians. The primary Assyrian god was Ashur. The second most powerful was Ishtar, the goddess of love, war, and procreation.

Archaeological excavations have provided evidence that the ancient Assyrians believed in a life after death. Like the Egyptian pharaohs who were buried with objects they believed they would need in the afterlife, Assyrians were buried with some of their favorite or most valued possessions, anything from swords to pottery. Wealthy Assyrians were laid to rest in a burial room they built, which is known as a mausoleum. The poor were buried in the ground near their homes. An oil lamp was placed at all the burial sites. Some speculate the light from the lamp was intended to help the soul see the way to the next world; others suggest it was to honor the dearly departed.

When it came to the sciences, the Assyrians were innovators. As was common in that era, illnesses were often seen as a punishment inflicted by the gods for some misdeed. But Assyrian physicians also understood that sickness could be caused by environmental factors, such as bad food. Cuneiform texts unearthed in Iran show that Assyrian doctors kept detailed written records, describing the patient's symptoms and past medical history. These tablets would be archived and used as a kind of medical journal, so doctors could research procedures performed by other healers. Some of the treatments included herbal drugs and changes in the patient's diet.

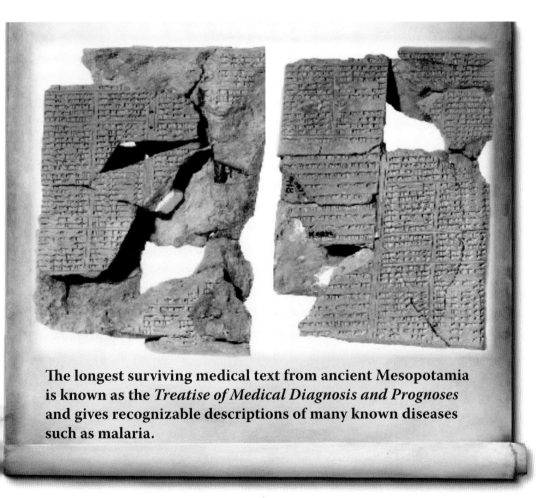

The longest surviving medical text from ancient Mesopotamia is known as the *Treatise of Medical Diagnosis and Prognoses* and gives recognizable descriptions of many known diseases such as malaria.

Assyria was also home to one of the ancient world's largest libraries. It was established centuries before the famous library at Alexandria, Egypt, and may have served as its inspiration. Established by King Ashurbanipal, who ruled between 668–627 BCE, the library was located in his Nineveh palace. It was eventually buried by invaders but was never really destroyed or burned, enabling many of the tablets to survive at least in part.

The Library of Ashurbanipal was found by British archeologist Austen Henry Layard between 1845 and 1851 during his excavations at Nineveh. The library included more than 25,000 cuneiform tablet fragments, detailing around 1,200 distinct texts. The topics included religion, government bureaucracy, science, math, poetry, and medical information. There were dictionaries and cultural writings such as proverbs and prayers, and historical records such as lists of regional rulers and sensitive government documents. Ashurbanipal also acquired texts from neighboring cultures, such as the famous Sumerian poem *Epic of Gilgamesh.*

Like modern libraries, Ashurbanipal's library was divided into rooms designated by topic. Each group of tablets indicated its subject matter. And throughout his reign, the king had a large contingent of scribes continually adding to the library.

The Assyrians were accomplished engineers, building roads throughout their empire to improve transportation. That led to the establishment of a kind of postal service by implementing messenger relay stations that gave them one of the most efficient communication systems of the ancient world.

Astrology was an important science for the Assyrians, who tried to connect events around them with the movement of the stars. Through their astrological knowledge, the Assyrians created an accurate yearly calendar that enabled them to predict eclipses and other natural events. Assyrian mathematicians were the first to divide a circle into 360 degrees and they were among the first to develop the concept of longitude and latitude for use in navigation.

While the military brought Assyria its wealth and power, its system of agriculture provided prosperity and stability. The fertile land between the rivers supported many food crops including apples, figs, olives, pomegranates, almonds, barley, wheat, and rice. Onions were also plentiful but were considered peasant food and were not eaten by the higher classes.

Most of the clothing worn by average Assyrians—generally knee-length tunics—was made of wool. However, garments worn by the king and other nobles or aristocracy were made from linen.

Hunting was also popular. Citizens were only allowed to hunt small game, while big game such as elephants, antelopes, and wild horses were strictly for the king and high officials. Mastiffs were often used to help in the hunt.

The garb of a king

One of the more unusual pastimes of the aristocracy was a type of polo. Rather than using horses, players rode on the shoulders of their playing partner.

Blessed with moderate weather, plentiful natural resources, reliable food resources, and scientific and medical knowledge that was especially advanced for its time, even the poorest of Assyrians experienced a relatively secure life. They enjoyed singing songs, often sung accompanied by an oud, an early stringed instrument similar to a lute. Songs were passed down orally from adults to children for centuries until many were eventually written down. The songs were important because they typically described important historical events and proved to be invaluable to modern historians in recreating daily life during the time of the Assyrian Empire.

Assyrian Healers

Assyrian healer

Assyria had an advanced medical system, although some of their perceptions toward illnesses were influenced more by their religious beliefs than hard science. While it was recognized that some organs could simply malfunction, many times illnesses were believed to be caused by evil spirits. As a result there were two types of medical healers: ashipu and asu.

According to the Iran Chamber Society, "One of the most important roles of the ashipu was to diagnose the ailment. In the case of internal diseases or difficult cases the ashipu determined which god or demon was causing the illness. He also attempted to determine if the disease was the result of some error or sin on the part of the patient."[1]

The ashipu treated patients with prayer or charms in order to drive out the spirit causing the disease. But Assyrians also used a more doctor-like healer called an asu, who used herbal remedies, dressed wounds, and also performed minor surgical procedures, such as draining fluid from the chest of pneumonia patients.

Some of the treatments used by Assyrian asu are not that dissimilar from modern medical procedures. For example, an asu treated headaches by crushing adaru-poplar seeds, which contain salicylic acid—a drug similar to modern-day aspirin, which has acetylsalicylic acid as its active ingredient. Similarly, many of the ointments, or plasters, they applied to wounds were made with heated plant resin or animal fat with alkali—ingredients that make soap. So when applied to a wound, these treatments would have helped to prevent infection.

Alexander's troops burning and looting the main palace in Persepolis, the capital of Persian Empire.

Legacy

The fall of the Assyrian Empire at the hands of the Babylonians did not mean the end of the Assyrian people, who were mostly the peasant farmers who worked the land between the Tigris and Euphrates Rivers. According to the book *The Might that Was Assyria,* "descendants of the Assyrian peasants would, as opportunity permitted, build new villages over the old cities and carried on with agricultural life, remembering traditions of the former cities."[1]

Within a few decades, the Assyrians became part of the Persian Empire. It is believed the Persians originally came to the Middle East from Central Asia around 1200 BCE. They settled in what is modern-day Iran and their civilization grew over the next 600 years. They eventually developed the military power to start conquering their neighbors around 600 BCE. Under Persian rule, it is believed the Assyrians were allowed to govern themselves and through their agriculture, the area where they lived became one of the wealthiest in the Persian Empire. As long as they paid taxes and tributes to the Persian leaders, they were left alone. That arrangement lasted until 330 BCE when Alexander the Great conquered Persia.

Assyrians were among the first cultures to accept Christianity. The Assyrian Church of the East was founded in 33 AD, a few years after Christ had been crucified, and by the third century AD the ancient god Ashur was no longer worshipped. Even after Muslims conquered Mesopotamia in the seventh century, the Assyrians retained their Christian religion and their language.

Over the succeeding centuries, the Assyrian people suffered at the hands of various invaders. The Ottoman Empire of Turkey declared a holy war, or *jihad,* against its Christian subjects, including the Assyrians, prior to World War I in the early 20th century. The Turkish army invaded northwestern Iran and committed terrible atrocities against the Assyrians and other populations, in what amounted to an attempt at ethnic genocide. The Assyrians lost nearly 70 percent of their population and the majority of their homeland in northern Mesopotamia during the World War I occupation by the Turks. Many Assyrians fled the oppression and now there are Assyrian communities in countries around the world, including the United States.

Not having a designated country makes it difficult for people today to explore Assyria's past firsthand, the way we can explore other ancient civilizations such as the Greeks, Egyptians, or Chinese. Part of the problem is political. Sites located in Iran are currently off-limits to Americans because of our lack of diplomatic ties with the country.

For example, outside Elam, Iran, there are inscriptions and carvings on a mountainside in Gol Gol village. Dating back 3,000 years, the carving shows an Assyrian soldier wearing a helmet while holding an arrow, with a moon and a star overhead. The site also has inscriptions written in cuneiform.

Visitors can also travel to Nineveh, located on the Tigris River in Iraq outside of modern Mosul. Nineveh, the third and final capital of Assyria, contains bas-reliefs dating back to the eighth century BCE. But until the political situation changes, this site and others will be inaccessible to most Westerners.

The parts of ancient Assyria located within Turkey were previously largely decimated. Those that weren't are not always protected. For example, Ziyaret Tepe was an ancient Assyrian city on the Tigris in what is now southeastern Turkey. It's considered a very important archaeological site because the city was a provincial capital. But it will be destroyed once

Assyrian Lamassu ("bull-man") statues from the throne room of Ashurbanipal in the British Museum.

construction of the Ilisu Dam is finished, perhaps as early as 2015, and the area becomes submerged.

Thanks to the archeological excavations by Austen Layard, the British Museum in London has one of the world's largest collections of Assyrian artifacts. Two galleries are devoted to Assyria, including cuneiform, tablets, sculptures, bas-reliefs, and stone panels from the Northwest Palace of King Ashurnasirpal II (who ruled from 883–859 BCE), which was built at Nimrud.

Although they do not have an established country, Assyrians remain a tight-knit culture, bound by their shared history and culture. They are divided into five religious sects: Church of the East, Chaldean, Maronite,

Assyrian children today, looking toward the future.

Syriac Orthodox, and Syriac Catholic. Despite their denominational differences, they remain united culturally. Just as Jews may belong to Orthodox or Reform synagogues, they are all still culturally Jewish. Or in the United States, some people are politically Republicans, Democrats, or independent. Yet they are all Americans. Likewise, even though they have no country, Assyrians continue to see themselves as a nation, a modern link to one of the greatest ancient civilizations ever seen on earth.

Genetics

DNA strand

For years, it was assumed that modern Syrians were descendants of the ancient Assyrians, if for no other reason than the similarity of the names. But geneticists now use modern technology to conduct DNA studies that can help determine a population's family tree. Many findings have been surprising, especially in light of modern political and ethnic tensions.

According to Luigi Luca Cavalli-Sforza, a professor of genetics at Stanford University, research has indicated that modern Assyrians in Iran are highly homogeneous. This means that as a people, they have a distinct DNA profile that is distinguishable from other population groups, such as Iranians, Syrians, Armenians, or Arabs.

Cavalli-Sforza's book also reports that modern Syrians are actually genetically closest to Jews, not modern Assyrians. Actually, Palestinians and Syrians are so closely genetically related to Jews as to be considered from the same population group, anthropologically speaking.

From a historical perspective, this leads Cavalli-Sforza and his associates to say that modern Assyrians are "believed to originate from the land of Assyria…and are possibly bona fide descendants of their namesakes."[2]

To conduct their study, the authors selected only populations that had been in the same geographic area for at least 500 years. Assyrians were one of the 491 populations identified. A population is identified by certain characteristics such as a shared language as well as common cultural, religious, social, and geographic features—the same aspects by which they distinguish themselves from other groups. Cavalli-Sforza's study showed populations were also identifiable by their genetic character, suggesting that even modern enemies may have far more in common than they realize.

Ancient Recipe: Baklava

Baklava is a very popular desert throughout the Middle East. Some believe that it was first created by the Assyrians sometime during the eighth century BC; others credit the Turks. Whatever its origin, it was a favorite Assyrian dish. A simple desert, it is made by sprinkling chopped nuts between thin layers of bread dough, adding some honey, then baking it. Even so, it was usually only prepared for special occasions. For many centuries it was also considered a wealthy person's delicacy.[1]

INGREDIENTS

3   cups coarsely ground walnuts
¼   cup sugar
1   teaspoon cinnamon
24 sheets phyllo dough (1 lb. box), thawed
½   teaspoon ground cloves

INGREDIENTS FOR SYRUP

1½ cups water
1½ cups sugar
¾   cup honey
1   cinnamon stick
½   sliced lemon with peel
Peel of ½ orange
5   whole cloves

Prepare ingredients before unwrapping the phyllo dough. It is very thin and delicate, so work with one sheet at a time, keeping the rest covered with a damp cloth or plastic wrap to prevent it from drying out.

DIRECTIONS

1. In a medium bowl, combine the nuts, ground cinnamon, cloves, and sugar.
2. Brush the bottom of a 9 x 13 pan with melted butter.
3. Bottom crust: Working with one sheet at a time, brush 8 sheets of phyllo pastry with butter and stack them in the pan, one on top of another. Sprinkle ½ cup of the nut mixture over the eighth sheet.
4. Center: Place 2 buttered sheets of phyllo on top and sprinkle another ½ cup of the nut mixture over it. Repeat 4 more times for a total of 10 sheets for the filling.
5. Top crust: Brush 6 phyllo sheets with butter just as you did with the bottom layer and stack them on top.
6. Cut through all the layers in a diamond pattern with a very sharp knife. Bake at 300° until golden brown, about one hour.
7. Combine all syrup ingredients in a medium saucepan and bring to a boil. Reduce the heat for 10 to 15 minutes. Strain and cool.
8. Remove the baklava from the oven and pour the cooled syrup evenly over the top.

Ancient Craft: Assyrian Bow & Arrow

The ancient Assyrians were excellent archers. You can easily make a replica of their bow and arrows.

SUPPLIES

½ inch PVC pipe, 42 inches long (The hardware store will cut it for you.)
½ inch PVC rounded pipe caps
½ inch pipe insulator
38 inches of nylon string
Your choice of colored duct tape
Electrical tape
Dowels cut 22 inches long

DIRECTIONS

1. Wrap the PVC pipe in duct tape.
2. Cut a one-inch notch into both ends of the pipe. Again, you can ask the hardware store to make the cut.
3. Stand in the middle of the pipe and bend it into an arc.
4. Cut a 4-½ inch length of pipe insulation and center it on the pipe.
5. Tightly wrap the electrical tape around the center of the insulation.
6. Wrap more tape tightly between the center tape and each edge so you end up with three ridges.
7. Now wrap the entire length of insulation in electrical tape.
8. Tie a knot on each end of string. Add a dab of super glue to secure the knot.
9. Slide the string into the slit on one end so the knot is inside the pipe.
10. Bend the pipe and slide the other end of the string into the other end of pipe.
11. Add the PVC caps to each end.
12. Add notches to one end of the dowels and use as arrows.

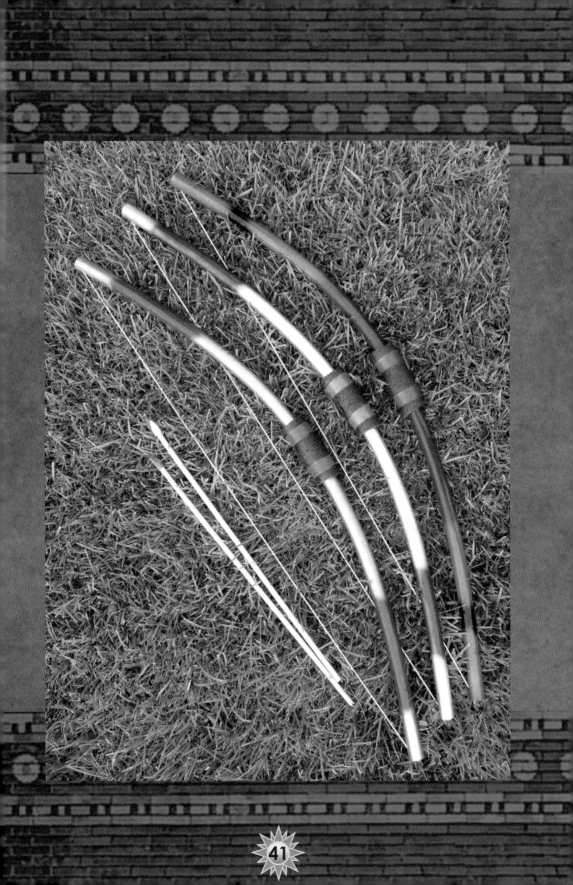

Timeline

All Dates BCE

5000	The earliest known settlement of Nineveh
4750	The first temple of Ashur is built, marking the beginning of the Assyrian calendar
2371	Sargon of Akkad establishes the first Assyrian kingdom in southern Mesopotamia
2000	Tin and textiles are the main trade commodities for Assyria
1900	Assur is founded
1765	The Code of Hammurabi created in Babylon
1680	Hurrians occupy Assyria
1400	Assyria regains its independence
1391	Moses born
1341	Egyptian King Tut dies at the age of 18
1307	Adadnarari establishes the first Assyrian Empire
1250	Shalmaneser I of Assyria conquers the kingdom of Mitanni
1220	Babylon comes under Assyrian control

British Museum's Assyrian art

Chapter One   The Battle of Carchemish
1. 2 Kings 23:29
http://bible.cc/2_kings/23-29.htm

2. 2 Chronicles 35:20-24
http://bible.cc/2_chronicles/35-20.htm

3. Genesis 2:8-14
http://bible.cc/genesis/2-8.htm

Chapter Two   Brief History
1. Robert A. Guisepi, Ancient Sumeria
http://history-world.org/sumeria.htm

Chapter Three   Law and Order
1. Fordham University, The Code of the Assura, c. 1075 BCE
http://www.fordham.edu/halsall/ancient/1075assyriancode.asp

2. Code of Hammurabi
http://www.commonlaw.com/Hammurabi.html

3. Ibid.

Chapter Four   Daily Life
1. Price, Massoume. Iran Chamber Society, *History of Ancient Medicine in Mesopotamia & Iran,* October 2001
    http://www.iranchamber.com/history/articles/ancient_medicine_mesopotamia_iran.php

Chapter Five   Legacy
1. Henry Saggs, *The Might that was Assyria* (London: Sidgwick & Jackson, 1984), p. 290.

2. Luigi Luca Cavalli-Sforza, Paolo Menozzi and Alberto Piazza, *The History and Geography of Human Genes* (Princeton, New Jersey: Princeton University Press, 1994), p. 243.

Ancient Recipe
1. *Assyrian Times,* "Baklava war intensifies between Turks and Greeks," May 15, 2006
    http://www.assyriatimes.com/engine/modules/news/article.php?storyid=3204

Books

Cavalli-Sforza, Luigi Luca and Paolo Menozzi and Alberto Piazza, *The History and Geography of Human Genes.* Princeton, New Jersey: Princeton University Press, 1994.

Luckenbill, Daniel David. *Ancient Records of Assyria and Babylonia.* Chicago: University of Chicago Press, 1968.

Olmstead, Albert. *History of Assyria.* Chicago: University of Chicago Press, 1960.

Saggs, Henry. *The Might That Was Assyria.* London: Sidgwick & Jackson, 1984.

On the Internet

Strabo, *Geography*

http://www.perseus.tufts.edu/hopper/text?doc=Perseus:text:1999.01.0198

Image: Hanging Gardens of Babylon, by Maarten van Heemskerck

http://www.cosmolearning.com/images/hanging-gardens-of-babylon-by-marten-van-heemskerck-935/

Robert A. Guisepi. Ancient Sumeria.

http://history-world.org/sumeria.htm

Fordham University, The Code of the Assura, c. 1075 BCE

http://www.fordham.edu/halsall/ancient/1075assyriancode.asp

Code of Hammurabi

http://www.commonlaw.com/Hammurabi.html

Price, Massoume. *History of ancient Medicine in Mesopotamia & Iran.* Iran Chamber Society, October 2001.

http://www.iranchamber.com/history/articles/ancient_medicine_mesopotamia_iran.php

"Baklava war intensifies between Turks and Greeks," *Assyria Times,* May 15, 2006.

http://www.assyriatimes.com/engine/modules/news/article.php?storyid=3204

Books

Matthews, Rupert. *You Wouldn't Want to Be an Assyrian Soldier!: An Ancient Army You'd Rather Not Join.* Clermont, Florida: Paw Prints Publishing, 2008.

Mayfield, Christine and Kristine M. Quinn. *Mesopotamia: World Cultures Through Time.* Huntington Beach, California: Teacher Created Materials, 2008.

Scholl, Elizabeth. *Ancient Mesopotamia.* Hockessin, Delaware. Mitchell Lane, 2009.

Schomp, Virginia. *Ancient Mesopotamia: The Sumerians, Babylonians, and Assyrians.* Danbury, Connecticut: Children's Press, 2008.

Steele, Phillip and Lorna Oakes. *Everyday Life in Egypt and Mesopotamia.* Leicester, United Kingdom: Anness, 2006.

Web Sites

Ancient Mesopotamia for Kids, The Assyrians

    http://mesopotamia.mrdonn.org/assyria.html

Assyrians – History for Kids

    http://www.historyforkids.org/learn/westasia/history/assyrians.htm

Assyrians – Social Studies for Kids, Assyrians

    http://www.socialstudiesforkids.com/wwww/world/assyriansdef.htm

Assyrian Empire – World History for Kids

    http://www.kidspast.com/world-history/0055-assyrian-empire.php

Assyria Online

    http://www.aina.org/aol/

archived (AHR-kived) – something stored; a collection of records

bas-relief (bah-ree-LEEF) – a stone sculpture in which the form being depicted extends only slightly from the surrounding surface and nothing is undercut

capital punishment (CAP-ih-tuhl PUN-ish-ment) – the legal killing of someone as punishment for a crime

delta (DELL-tuh) – the triangular tract of sediment deposited at the mouth of a river

demographics (dem-oh-GRAF-icks) – the characteristics of a population, such as ethnic makeup and age

innovators (IN-no-vay-tehrs) – people who create new things

lute (LEWT) – a guitar-like stringed instrument having a body shaped like a pear

mastiff (MASS-tiff) – a breed of large dogs

mausoleum (maw-zuh-LEE-uhm) – a building above ground in which the dead are buried

puppet king (PUH-puht king) – a ruler who is installed by an imperial power to keep the appearance of local authority

sack (SACK) – destroy

Semitic (suh-MIH-tick) – people whose origins are in the Arabian Peninsula and surrounding region

stele (STEE-lee) – an upright stone with an inscribed or sculptured surface

theocracy (thee-AH-cruh-see) – a system of government in which priests rule in the name of their god or gods

ziggurat (ZIG-uh-rat) – a rectangular stepped tower

Index